My Mother Loved Tea

The Story of Ruth Bigelow and how she changed the way Americans enjoy tea.

By David C. Bigelow

Dedication

This book is dedicated to my
mother and father, and all the
many men and women, both
past and present, both inside
as well as outside our company,
who through their hard work and
dedication made the Bigelow
Tea Company what it is today.

In many ways this is their story.
We hope it brings back fond
memories. It's full of the many
ups and downs—mostly ups,
thank goodness—that we went
through. It's remarkable when
one looks back how many times
fate stepped in to point us in a
new and positive direction.

Although you won't see any
names—the list is very, very
long—everyone is there in spirit.
We want to thank each person
for their unique contribution. We
have made this journey together
as one big family. It has been one
of great love and perseverance.
This book is their story just as
much as it is ours.

The Bigelow Family

Table of Contents

R.C. Bigelow Company History 1

It all began in 1945 3

A Defining Moment 19

Eunice and David Bigelow 35

In Remembrance… 39

A New Era and Business Doubles 41

Revolutionary Packaging… A fresh cup of Tea 49

The Charleston Tea Plantation 61

How Tea Is Made 67

The History of Tea 75

Tea is Healthy 83

One More Way… My Mother Loved Tea 84

More Ways for You to Love Our Tea 86

In Closing 94

ISBN 978-0-9793431-9-3
Printed in Canada through
Benjamin Press

$\mathcal{I}$n 1945, Ruth and David Bigelow, Sr. had a dream. Their dream was to start their own food business, to work for themselves instead of others and to be independent. They also wanted to be able to pass this on to their son David and his family.

This is the story of that dream… and how it became a reality… a reality way beyond their wildest dreams…

R.C. Bigelow Company History

By David C. Bigelow

Ruth Campbell Bigelow, the Creator of "Constant Comment"® the one single tea that would revolutionize the way Americans enjoy tea.

Little would my mother, Ruth Bigelow, ever have imagined when she created "Constant Comment"® over sixty years ago that this one single tea would revolutionize the way Americans enjoy tea.

Truth was that in 1945, the tea section of the typical grocery store contained only black tea. It came in large boxes with lots of tea bags and lots of brand names, but however you sliced and diced it, it was all the same… black tea. Believe it or not, there was no such thing as a specialty tea to be found and in Ruth Bigelow's mind, this was wrong. She felt that tea drinkers deserved more. She felt that they would enjoy a tea that was smoother in taste and more flavorful. Time would prove her right. But the path to success was not an easy one.

Ruth Campbell Bigelow

It all began in 1945

To a great degree, Bigelow Tea was a business born of necessity. Both my mother and my father had had successful careers in the 1920's, she as one of New York City's more outstanding interior decorators and he in the publishing industry. But the depression of '29, took a terrible toll on their business lives. My father lost his job at McGraw Hill in the early thirties. He would spend the next eight years on a variety of small business ventures. My mother's decorating business declined sharply as her wealthy clients' financial misfortunes seriously reduced their needs for her services.

In the early forties, it became clear to my mother that a change of business direction was necessary. After some thirty years of decorating, she made the decision to go into the food business. Unlike decorating where each new client required that you start from scratch to learn their tastes and requirements, she felt that if she could create a successful food product, one that people wanted over and over again, the need to constantly re-invent herself would go away.

As the decorating business had sharply declined during the thirties, my mother had been forced to move her showroom from a prestigious two story shop on 72nd Street and Madison Avenue, first renting at a location on 52nd Street between Park and Lexington and then later on 57th Street. In the early 1940's, my parents set out to find a more permanent home where they could begin their new business, the two of them walking up and down local streets in mid-town Manhattan. They discovered a brownstone at 241 East 60th Street owned by two sisters who had let the building fall into serious disrepair. Dipping into the last of their life's savings, they bought the

The Brownstone on 60th Street where it all began.

Chinese seasoning labels

building and began with their own hands to replaster and paint, to build a home for themselves, a place to start their new business.

Their new building (four stories) featured two showroom windows on the first two floors and my mother once again put her logo "Ruth Campbell Bigelow, Interiors" in large gold leaf letters across the window on the second floor. The large room behind this window would become not only her new office but with my father's desk somewhat side by side to hers, they would begin R.C. Bigelow, Inc.

The entrepreneurial spirit that these two brought to their new venture was truly remarkable. My father, by now retired and almost seventy, and my mother at fifty with some thirty years of decorating behind her, both added a wealth of business knowledge to this effort. The question—what product could they make – where could they start?

*Our first piece of equipment –
The chinese seasoning blender.*

They knew where they were going to make it. On the ground floor of the new building behind the showroom window was a room some fourteen-feet wide by twenty-feet deep – with a separate door that led out to the street. Through this door would pass all receiving and shipping for the next five years. The room would be their manufacturing home. The basement with its dirt floor and timbered posts would be the warehouse. As impossible as this sounds, somehow they would make it work.

As for their first product, it would be Chinese Seasoning – a mixture of salt, milk sugar and glutamate. This decision came from a number of years of talking with many of the major milling companies of the time and discovering that glutamate was the secret ingredient used by every Chinese restaurant to give their food lots of flavor. Their first customer was a wholesaler to those very restaurants, the Wing Tuck Trading Company on Mulberry Street in Chinatown.

And so they bought a small blender and began to bring in barrels of glutamate and 100 pound bags of salt and milk sugar. With a hand crank lift to enable them to raise the ingredients up to the top of the blender, and with the assistance of one employee, they began the process of blending and packing their new product in 2 ½ lb. cans, 35 lb. tins and 50 lb. drums. When each order was completed, they would ship it to Chinatown, sometimes even taking it themselves in the family car. Needless to say, they did all the buying of their materials, labels, containers, corrugated, etc. They did all their own costing, pricing and billing.

The percent of glutamate in the blend, was a key issue in quality control. My mother and dad, of course, guaranteed it, and it was probably the reason they got the business because they were so honest. With all the ingredients being pure white (salt, $.06/lb., milk sugar, $.10/lb., and glutamate, $1.45/lb.) it would have been very easy to go light on the expensive ingredient, glutamate. But with my mother and father, their honesty was implicit and this was undoubtedly recognized by the customer. Wing Tuck Trading proved to be an excellent distributor and his orders for the seasoning powder were what kept us in business for those first few years.

With me away at college, my mother and father ran the business like this for the first three years of its existence. Along the way, they expanded their customer base to include some of the

BIGELOW'S

Happiness

BRAND

TAPIOCA

Fully Prepared–Add Only Water

NET WT.   12½ OZS.   354,369 GMS.

DISTRIBUTED BY
R.C. BIGELOW, INC.
241 E. 60th St., New York, N.Y.
MADE IN U.S.A.

BIGELOW'S

Happiness

BRAND

TAPIOCA

is delicious in flavor, healthful, nutritious and energizing for both children and grown-ups.

HAPPINESS TAPIOCA

HAPPINESS TAPIOCA

is fully prepared - add only water.

Ruth Bigelow
reading her
fan mail

Original "Constant Comment"® glass jar

large New York wholesalers at that time. They also cornered the tapioca market briefly at the end of World War II by buying the first shipments to come in from the Far East in over five years . . . an effort which would see the two of them spending their evenings picking out the sticks and stones that came in the tapioca bales on a make shift chute and packing the product into 5 lb. canisters for customers like the Waldorf Astoria.

With my mother still spending some part of every day on her decorating business, she turned her attention to her first love, tea. From a longtime friend, she had heard about a tea that was popular in the South during Colonial times. The recipe, she was told, had called for tea to be blended with orange peel and sweet spice. This sounded so good to her that she decided to try and recreate it. After weeks of experimentation in her kitchen, she came up with a blend that totally intrigued her as well as many of her friends and acquaintances. As a matter of fact, her tea was served by one of those friends at a social occasion who reported back to her that "Ruth, your tea caused nothing but constant comments." My mother, searching for a name for her new discovery, promptly jumped on the "Constant Comment"®, feeling that it aptly implied that her tea was popular and everybody was talking about it. Although many people in those early days and even years later felt that this name was not descriptive enough, Mom felt strongly that this was the name she wanted. Time would once again prove her so correct.

"Constant Comment"®
fine tea flavored with
golden orange peel
and sweet spice.
The true original.

Their first package was to be a small glass jar and during this period (1946 – 47) a famous event was to occur which later would give a direction to the company without which it probably would never have succeeded. As the story goes, my mother was attempting to sell her tea to a grocer one day and he was not buying her sales pitch. "I have never heard of your product. I have never had any calls for it and until I do, I'm sorry but I can't carry it" was what she was

The turning point.

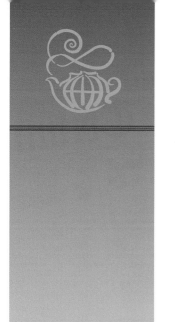

hearing as the grocer kept running off to get products (pre self-service times) for the customer standing alongside her. And it is this customer, whose name we will never know, that asked the key question "What is this product that you're trying to sell?" Mom, who must have been somewhat relieved to hear at least some interest in her new creation, unscrewed the cap of the little glass jar and the customer proceeded not only to look at "Constant Comment"® but also take a whiff of it. The wonderful aroma did the trick. She promptly decided to buy a jar.

So the unwilling grocer had made his first sale but he hadn't changed his tune. My mother had brought six jars with her and the grocer, in some exasperation because he was so busy, told her to leave the other jars and call him the following week. When she did so the story was still the same "no demand, no sale" and so she offered to come and get the balance of the tea she had left. Well, said the grocer, "that won't be necessary" and when she asked why, the grocer said "Oh, the lady who bought the jar while you were in the store came back later and bought the other five." Whether the grocer was ever billed for the six jars, we don't know. In all likelihood, he probably wasn't. Although on the surface, this story seems like one of success mixed with ultimate failure, remember that in failure very often can be found an idea that later leads to success.

In any event, shortly after this time, the little glass jar went away to be replaced by a four ounce canister of loose tea. To decorate this container, they wrapped it in gold foil. The label featured a tiny little picture of two ladies having tea with the name "Constant Comment"® written just below them. During this time, mom had been fortunate enough to place her new creation in a few of Manhattan's finer stores – most importantly it was on the shelves at

My father painted the ladies dresses red and the background green.

Mom's hand painted
sales material.

Bloomingdales, New York's most prestigious department store for those looking for finer foods in the city. Other names included Charles & Co. who had several locations in Manhattan and B. Altmans Department Store.

Sales were very slow. Only a few small batches of "Constant Comment"® tea were required to be produced every month. To stimulate sales, they had decided that my dad would add a little extra color to the sepia colored label by painting the dresses of the two ladies red and the background green. Not known for his artistic ability, the color nevertheless was a distinct improvement to an otherwise very plain label. He usually did this job in the evening and it was during one of those sessions while I was sitting with him that he said to me, "Son, don't tell your mother, but I don't think this tea is ever going to go anywhere." Although normally quite a good predictor of future events, my dad fortunately proved wrong in this instance.

My mother, with no money available for advertising, also began in the evenings to create hand painted flyers extolling the virtues of "Constant Comment"® and listing a store in the city where it could be found. These she would mail out to people whose names appeared in the social columns of the New York Herald Tribune. This was to be the first advertising that the Bigelow Company ever did and it must have piqued some interest from those who received them because sales at the various stores picked up once she began.

Dad and myself circa 1951.

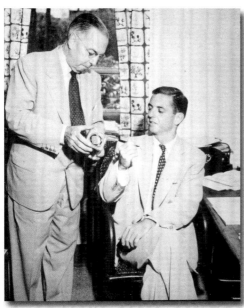

And the N.Y. Herald Tribune also made a gigantic contribution to the future success of "Constant Comment"® at this time in the form of a feature article written by their then famous food editor, Clementine Paddleford. In it, she told the whole story of how "Constant Comment"® had come to be as well as the names of the stores in Manhattan where it could be

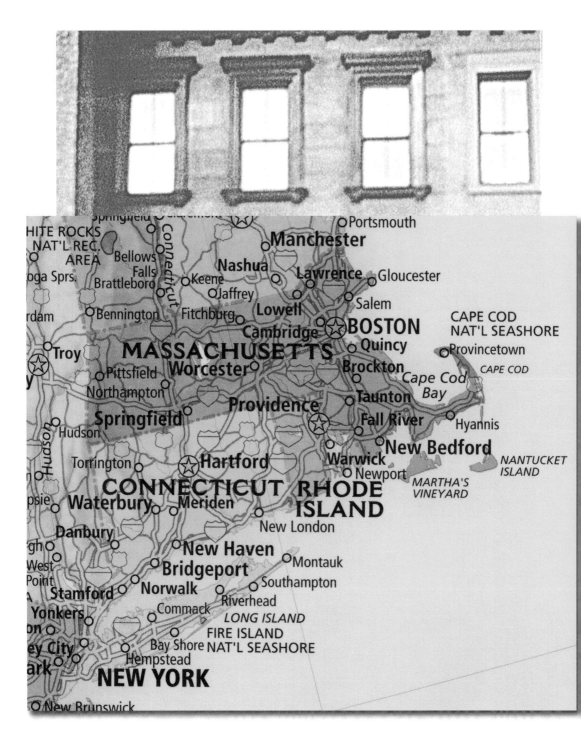

Our first sales territory.

purchased. Not only did many thousands of readers see the story but it also helped to validate what mom and dad were doing.

It was around this time that another very important event took place that was to definitely have a major impact on the future of the young company. Still feeling that grocery stores were where "Constant Comment" should be, my father wrote a food broker and good friend in Boston, asking if he would be interested in carrying "Constant Comment" and offering it to the New England grocery stores. The firm was one of Boston's biggest food brokerage concerns carrying many major brands. It would have been a great feather in their cap had they been able to secure the services of such a fine firm.

But, it was here that fate stepped in when his friend wrote back and explained that "Constant Comment" was way too small a product for them to carry and besides, he felt sure that "Constant Comment" would most certainly fail for lack of consumer knowledge and demand. Instead, he recommended a commission sales representative who sold to gift shops, department stores and gourmet shops. My father's friend felt these types of stores would be vastly better outlets for the fledgling "Constant Comment". As it turned out, this was exactly the good advice that was needed at this juncture as future events would soon show.

And so it was that this representative was contacted and in due course agreed to represent "Constant Comment". Small orders began to flow in from a wide variety of specialty accounts across the New England states, particularly gift shops.

In 1948, I graduated from college and joined the firm. I would spend my first year helping with the blending and packing of the Chinese Seasoning, doing costing,

Small orders began to flow in from a wide variety of specialty accounts across the New England states, particularly gift shops.

The original "Constant Comment" package.

The 2 oz. canister (circa 1950's).

The 4 oz. canister (circa 1950's).

and making deliveries to Chinatown. A lot of time would also be spent trying to develop additional customers for the seasoning. In the process, I would learn that the seasoning business required a lot of time to secure a new account, brought in very small volume and was marginally profitable. In addition, a competitor could steal an account for just a few cents per pound. The tea business, where brand loyalty amongst thousands of consumers could be developed over time, seemed the much better way to go.

As a first step, we decided to change the "Constant Comment" label. A new 2 oz. loose tea size would be added to the existing 4 oz. size. We felt the new package needed to be more descriptive so we added the line "Tea flavored with rind of oranges and sweet spice." We chose the color red because we felt it would be eye catching. As it turned out, many of the characteristics of that package can still be seen in the "Constant Comment" package of today.

Our "Constant Comment" package today.

Early Counter Card

A Defining Moment

In 1949, our New England sales representative paid a visit to the company. His purpose was to announce that he was resigning the line. The reason: "Constant Comment" was not doing well in the gift shops that he had sold it to in New England. All of us were confounded. Our infant tea business was about to suffer a mortal blow. If "Constant Comment" wasn't selling in New England gift shops, what chance did it have anywhere else? We asked him to give us a little time, which he agreed to, and then we put our heads together to see if we could find a solution.

As we pondered, we remembered mom's day with the grocer and the customer. What was the key element that had caused that customer to buy that first bottle of "Constant Comment" Tea? The answer: she had not only *seen* the product with the dramatic orange peel mixed in with the tea but she had also *smelled* the wonderful orange and spice aroma. Could it be that we could create a jar that would invite people to "open and whiff"? Would that do the trick? We still had a number of cases of the little glass jars that had been "Constant Comment"s first package. Why not give it a try? And so we did. We sent about a dozen jars to our sales representative, each with a small "Constant Comment" label on the side of the jar, an invitation to "Open and Whiff" label on the top, and half filled with tea. The results were immediate. He reported back within a month that in the stores where he had placed the whiffing jars, "Constant Comment" was selling briskly and the storeowners were quite pleased.

Whiffing Jar

An early merchandising shelf rack.

This truly was the moment the Bigelow Tea Company was born. Had it not been for the "whiffing jar", the Bigelow Tea Company would never have succeeded. Based on its success in New England, we went on to create a "Get Acquainted" case which consisted of six, 4 oz. canisters, five, 2 oz. canisters and a "whiffing jar". The cost: $6.75 delivered anywhere in the U.S.A. Over the next ten years, the company would sell tens of thousands of these cases all across the country.

They say timing is everything. Certainly that was the case with "Constant Comment". It just so happened that in the late forties and early fifties, gift shops were very prevalent. Every town had at least one. Also, gourmet foods were just beginning to pique consumer interest and every gift shop had a "gourmet corner" with high priced herbs and spices, jams and jellies, cookies and crackers. "Constant Comment" with its cute little canisters and its unique "whiffing jar" fit in perfectly with this setting.

Ruth Bigelow and associates at Gift Trade Show (circa 1958).

In 1950, with tea now matching if not exceeding the Chinese Seasonings as an income producer, it was decided to move our infant business to Connecticut. This move would fulfill a dream for my mother and father, a dream to return to their Wilton, Connecticut home, a home they had owned since the twenties but had been forced to leave and rent in the mid 1930's because of the depression. They sold the brownstone and bought a small, two-story factory on Hoyt Street in Norwalk, CT. They put

The Hoyt Street factory.

half of their proceeds from the sale of the brownstone down on the new building and used the other half for working capital.

The sales force, which now numbered some ten to twelve gift shop representatives located strategically around the country, was busy sending in orders every day. The next few years would be uneventful as the business grew slowly but steadily.

By 1954, the company had a substantial customer base of several thousand stores. In addition to gift shops, "Constant Comment" was also being sold in hardware stores, beauty parlors, florists, gourmet food stores and department stores.

Because each manufacturer's representative covered such vast areas of the country with repeat calls possibly being months apart, mom devised a return mail pre-paid postage order form to be mailed monthly to the entire customer base (see page 24). To make the customer's life as easy as possible, one had only to fill out their name and address and fill in how many cases they required of each item. All else including product pictures, descriptions and wholesale prices were pre-printed on the form. In time, the monthly order forms became a great way to introduce new products and sell gift packs at the holidays. The order forms proved very popular with the trade and many, many thousands of orders were generated in this fashion over quite a few years.

In 1954, with the business doing well and my mother and father definitely on their way to financial security, I decided to leave the business and move to New York to pursue a long time interest in cinematography.

First production line in the Hoyt Street factory.

R. C. BIGELOW, INC. POSTAGE-FREE ORDER FORM

BILL TO: _____

ADDRESS _____

CITY _____ **STATE** _____ **ZIP** _____ **REPRESENTATIVE:** _____

SHIPPING DATE DESIRED: _____

SHIP TO:

ADDRESS _____ **STATE** _____ **ZIP** _____

CITY _____ **STATE** _____ **ZIP** _____

YOUR ORDER NO. _____ **TERMS: 1% — 10 DAYS, NET 30 DAYS** **PRICES: DELIVERED**

Two EXTRA ways to expand your sales of Bigelow "Constant Comment" Tea

Now your customers can enjoy the convenience of Instant Tea and Hot Tea and Toddy Mix.

"CONSTANT COMMENT" INSTANT TEA

QTY.	DESCRIPTION	CODE	CASE PACK	RETAIL	CASE COST
cases	1.25 oz. bottle	1712	12	$1.59	$12.72

"CONSTANT COMMENT" HOT TEA AND TODDY MIX

With lemon and sugar added

QTY.	DESCRIPTION	CODE	CASE PACK	RETAIL	CASE COST
cases	1.7 oz. envelope	1872	36	$ .29	$6.96
cases	14 oz. bottle	1812	12	1.59	12.72

When ordering "Constant Comment" Hot Tea and Toddy Mix, please make sure your total order (including other Bigelow products) is $50.00 or more. This $50.00 minimum applies only when ordering "Constant Comment" Hot Tea and Toddy Mix because of its weight and consequent high shipping costs.

BIGELOW "CONSTANT COMMENT" TEA

The famous delicious blend of fine tea flavored with rind of oranges and sweet spice

QTY.	DESCRIPTION	CODE	CASE PACK	RETAIL	CASE PRICE
	2 oz. loose tea	1502	12	$ .95	$7.60
cases	4 oz. loose tea	1504	12	1.69	13.52
cases	8 oz. loose tea	1508	6	3.15	12.60
cases	5 tea bags	1005	24	.35	6.50
cases	10 tea bags	1018	18	.65	7.80
cases	24 tea bags	1024	12	1.35	10.80
cases	50 tea bags	1050	6	2.09	8.36

BIGELOW CHINESE FORTUNE TEA

The same smooth-tasting blend you've enjoyed in fine Chinese restaurants

QTY.	DESCRIPTION	CODE	CASE PACK	RETAIL	CASE PRICE
cases	1½ oz. loose tea	3502	12	$ .95	$7.60
cases	5 tea bags	3005	24	.35	5.60
cases	10 tea bags	3010	18	.65	7.80
cases	20 tea bags	3020	6	.95	3.80

BIGELOW PLANTATION MINT TEA

A southern favorite. Fine tea refreshingly flavored with real garden mint.

QTY.	DESCRIPTION	CODE	CASE PACK	RETAIL	CASE PRICE
cases	1½ oz. loose tea	2502	12	$ .55	$7.60
cases	5 tea bags	2005	24	.35	5.60
cases	10 tea bags	2010	18	.65	7.80
cases	20 tea bags	2020	6	.95	3.80

"Constant Comment" Hot Tea Promotion

24 "Constant Comment" 5 tea bags free ($8.40 retail value) with every floor display. You make 38% profit with this time-tested promotion.

1

"CONSTANT COMMENT" ALL TEA BAGS
Code 1170

Contains:
40 10 tea bags
50 24 tea bags
48 5 tea bags (includes free goods!)

Total Delivered Cost $ 73.32
Retail Value 118.40

Please send _____ display(s)

2

"CONSTANT COMMENT" LOOSE TEA AND TEA BAGS
Code 1080

Contains:
20 2 oz. loose tea
20 4 oz. loose tea
90 10 tea bags
24 24 tea bags
12 50 tea bags
24 5 tea bags (free goods)

Total Delivered Cost $ 77.50
Retail Value 124.66

Please send _____ display(s)

3

THREE FLAVOR ALL TEA BAGS
Code 1230

"Constant Comment"
48 24 tea bags
24 5 tea bags (free goods)

Plantation Mint
24 5 tea bags

Chinese Fortune
24 5 tea bags

Total Delivered Cost $ 70.00
Retail Value 113.40

Please send _____ display(s)

4

THREE FLAVOR LOOSE TEA AND TEA BAGS
Code 1280

"Constant Comment"
12 2 oz. loose tea 12 24 tea bags
12 4 oz. loose tea 12 50 tea bags
20 10 tea bags 24 5 tea bags (free goods)

Plantation Mint
24 5 tea bags

Chinese Fortune
24 5 tea bags

Total Delivered Cost $ 73.56
Retail Value 118.76

Please send _____ display(s)

7010F

Dimensions: 62¼" high, 14" deep, 25½" wide.

Free goods offer effective September 1, 1970, ends March 31, 1971.

The monthly mail order form.

Bigelow GREAT TEAS OF THE WORLD

(ATTRACTIVE PRE-PACKED GREAT TEAS OF THE WORLD SHELF...)

QTY	DESCRIPTION	CODE	CASE PACK	RETAIL	CASE PRICE
cases	English Breakfast 20 tea bags	7030	6	.95	...
cases	English Breakfast 8 tea bags	6030	9	.49	...
cases	English Breakfast 4 oz. loose tea	8030	9	1.69	...
cases	Earl Grey 20 tea bags	7025	6	.95	...
cases	Earl Grey 8 tea bags	6025	9	.49	...
cases	Earl Grey 4 oz. loose tea	8025	9	1.69	...
cases	Darjeeling 20 tea bags	7020	6	.95	...
cases	Darjeeling 8 tea bags	6020	9	.49	...
cases	Darjeeling 4 oz. loose tea	8020	9	1.69	...
cases	Irish 20 tea bags	7015	6	.95	1.96
cases	Irish 8 tea bags	6015	9	.49	1.96
cases	Irish 4 oz. loose tea	8015	9	1.69	55.96
cases	Formosa Oolong 20 tea bags	7060	6	.95	3.80
cases	Formosa Oolong 8 tea bags	6035	9	.49	1.96
cases	Formosa Oolong 3½ oz. loose tea	8035	9	15.49	55.96
cases	Green 20 tea bags	7040	6	.95	1.96
cases	Green 8 tea bags	6040	9	.49	6.36
cases	Green 5 oz. loose tea	8040	9	1.59	3.80
cases	Ceylon Orange Pekoe 20 tea bags	7010	6	.95	1.96
cases	Ceylon Orange Pekoe 8 tea bags	6010	9	.49	6.36
cases	Ceylon Orange Pekoe 3½ oz. loose tea	8010	9	.95	3.80
cases	American Breakfast 20 tea bags	7005	6	.95	1.96
cases	American Breakfast 8 tea bags	6005	9	.49	1.96
cases	American Breakfast 5 oz. loose tea	8005	9	15.49	55.96

DIMENSIONS: 16" WIDE, 7¼" DEEP 8½" HIGH

As 1955 rolled around, an event was to take place that would truly test the strength of our new company. The event was a flood throughout the entire region triggered by a tropical system that settled over the Connecticut area and brought a drenching rain for many days. An extremely serious crisis loomed as rivers throughout the state overflowed their banks. By the fifth day, not only was the Norwalk River (which was 100 yards from our plant) a raging torrent, but everything in its path including trees, small buildings, etc. were floating down stream. As this great mass of material piled up at bridge crossings along the 30 mile route from Danbury to Norwalk, the bridges began to collapse one by one adding to the debris rushing down the river.

Flood of 1955 in Connecticut.

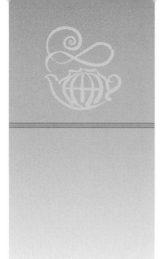

Just beyond our little factory stood the last obstruction, the Wall Street Bridge with four-story apartment buildings all across it. As the huge culvert beneath the bridge clogged up with debris, a vast lake began to form. With the Bigelow building being as close as it was, it wasn't long before we had six feet of water on the ground floor. The lake throughout downtown Norwalk above the bridge became huge.

The police, of course, evacuated everybody from the area in anticipation that the bridge could not hold out for long and sure enough, one night, with what must have been a mighty roar, the bridge and the apartment buildings all collapsed into Long Island Sound.

The day after the flood of 1955.

In that same instant, the back wall of our building also collapsed. The waters both in the building, as well as around it were also rushing toward the Sound. With it went everything on the ground floor, our production line, all raw materials and lots of cases of packed tea. Everything spilled out into the parking lot behind the building. Fortunately, because the support walls of the building were parallel to the direction the water took, our building remained standing. The second floor with all of our financial records was saved.

The following day when my folks were able to view the damage, the first question from my dad was "Can we be back in business by Monday?"

How many business owners at the age of 77, upon seeing their business almost totally destroyed, could ask that question? But that was my dad's mindset and I'm sure, my mother's also. They would go on. It took a bit longer than Monday morning, but in the following weeks (I returned to help out), we scoured all the mud from the walls and the floors, re-built the back wall, cleaned up the loose tea filler, set up the production tables and off they went again. The loss was uninsured, but their vendors stood tall, offering them open credit. "Pay us when you can" was what they heard. Mom and dad were able to get their tea, cans, labels, cartons and all the other things they needed. Within a few months, it was business as usual.

Although the business was able to resume, the center area of Norwalk that had been affected by the flood came

More flood damage to Hoyt Street building.

Merwin Street building, Norwalk, Connecticut.

under federal and state redevelopment. Mom and dad were told that in two years time, their building would fall under eminent domain. With redevelopment aid, they were able to buy a 100 year old Dutch style all brick factory about a mile away on Merwin Street. The new facility, the Mayhoff Dress & Shirt Factory as it was known, was actually a complex of several connected buildings. It had at one time been fully self sufficient with dormitories for some twenty seamstresses brought over from Ireland, a kitchen and dining hall, offices and, of course, a sky-lighted sewing room on the top floor in the back. With its beautiful rich facade and large dormer-like windows on the top floor in the front building, it was truly a classic of architecture. With many additions over time, it would be the home of Bigelow Tea for the next 33 years.

For several years, my parents had been buying "Constant Comment" tea bags from a contract tea packer on Long Island. The tea, stored in large tin pails, would be driven to their plant early in the morning in the family car (about an hour's trip). They would wait there while a tea bag machine made 50,000 tea bags and then bring them back, all packed in white cartons of 100 tea bags each. Once back at our factory, we would transfer them from the cartons and pack them by hand into ten tea bag and twenty-four tea bag size canisters. From a cost accountant's perspective, this was without a doubt, the most inefficient and costly way to be in the tea bag business, but that didn't bother my mom and dad. They could offer "Constant Comment" in tea bags and that's what they wanted!

Hand-packing tea bags into tins.

Our first tea bag machines.

"Constant Comment" tea bags proved very popular with consumers. In any case, now that they had this new building (they moved in 1957), they decided that they wanted their own tea bag machines. Having heard that Lipton was selling all their old machines, my mother and father went to the New Jersey Lipton plant, were treated very nicely by the Lipton folks, and promptly bought two used tea bag machines. From that time forward, we made all our own tea bags.

Something of a workaholic with her business almost constantly on her mind, my mother was continually generating new ideas. In the mid-fifties she came up with a winner. With more and more gift shops, gourmet shops, flower shops, hardware stores, beauty parlors, yes, all of those and more, selling "Constant Comment" Tea, we needed some way to tell people where they could find it. Her idea was to place little, tiny ads in small town

Ruth, David, Jr. and David, Sr.

A busy shipping dock at Merwin Street.

newspapers, "sign posts" if you will, directing people to the store in their town that carried "Constant Comment". Tied to the stores purchases and involving a mind-boggling internal filing system (no computers to help us then), literally thousands of ads would be run across America in the late fifties. Although the program was daunting in its complexity, to my mom, this program was essential and therefore worth the enormous amount of effort it would take to make it happen. Consumers were not the only beneficiaries. Stores loved it too because it helped to create more foot traffic for them. Like the "whiffing jar," this sign post ad campaign played a huge part in "Constant Comment"'s early success.

Early advertising

"Sign-Post" advertising

Eunice and David Bigelow

Eunice and David Bigelow

In 1959, my parents asked if I would come back to the business. They felt they were getting on in years and if I did not return they would be forced to sell the business.

I had married in the intervening years and my wife Eunice and I discussed this decision at length. I was somewhat reluctant at first as I had spent a lot of time and effort on a new direction in life, but Eunice encouraged me to rejoin the family business. She felt this was the right way to go.

When we returned, we found that the company was slowly evolving from the gift, gourmet and department store era into the supermarket era. As the 60's dawned, we began getting more and more inquiries from grocery stores. "Am getting calls for "Constant Comment". Please send price list," they read. The very thing that the original grocer my mother had called on so many years before had said, "I can't carry your product, because I don't get calls for it," was now happening. All those thousands of gift and gourmet shops selling all those tens of thousands of packages of "Constant Comment" to all those hundreds of thousands of

There is no question that Art Linkletter was an enormous help to us in getting "Constant Comment"® started in grocery stores and supermarkets.

people who not only bought it for themselves but also gave it as gifts, sending "Constant Comment" in many instances to friends and relatives in other cities and towns, had made it happen. The swell of demand for "Constant Comment", although still relatively small, was beginning to happen. But even with all this interest, when "Constant Comment" first appeared on grocers' shelves, the best it could muster was perhaps four facings -- a tiny entity surrounded by huge 100-count boxes of black tea. It was truly the first specialty tea to appear in grocery stores.

Needless to say, sales were very slow. The whiffing jar no longer had a place in a grocery store environment. We needed someone to come and speak for "Constant Comment" and we found it in the person of Art Linkletter. A decision was made to put "Constant Comment" on Art Linkletter's House Party on the CBS radio network. He worked miracles. In addition to Art speaking about "Constant Comment" every week, we also put his smiling face on a variety of our floor stands. There is no question that Art Linkletter was an enormous help to us in getting "Constant Comment" started in grocery stores and supermarkets.

Art Linkletter

Ruth and David Bigelow, Sr.

In Remembrance...

In 1966, after a long five year battle with cancer, my mother passed away. Despite the severity of her illness, she continued working right up until the end. A few years later, my father would also leave us at age 92. What they had achieved in their lifetime was absolutely remarkable.

If only they could come back and see their business as it is today. Were there a Hall of Fame for entrepreneurs, their names should be on the wall.

I have often said that it was fortunate that I wasn't there when they first began because I would have told them that there was no way they were going to succeed. What they had achieved would have been considered unattainable by most but by sheer will and a constant belief that they could do it, they had succeeded. The word failure was not in their vocabulary.

I'm glad they were able to see their infant company come of age. My mother had accomplished her goal. "Constant Comment" had broken the one flavor (black tea) "sound" barrier. Tea sections in grocery stores and supermarkets would never again be the same.

A competitor's Spiced Tea product.

A New Era and Business Doubles

In 1973, a strange and totally unexpected thing happened. As it turned out, it would prove quite providential to our future success. But when it first occurred, my wife and I were quite taken aback and *very concerned*. It just so happened that a package of spiced tea from one of our competitors came on the market that year that appearance-wise was a dead ringer for our "Constant Comment". People looking at both packages could barely tell them apart. This was obviously going to cause major confusion, with many consumers likely to pick up their package thinking it was ours. Everything we had worked so hard for all those years was threatened, and so, with our attorneys, we headed to court. There, at a pre-trial hearing, the story got even worse as their attorney revealed to the judge that their client was going to bring out additional teas in the near future with that *exact same look*. Imagine the shock that my wife and I both felt at this revelation! Leaving the courthouse, we queried our attorney as to what we should do—how could we handle this enormous encroachment on our company. His answer, "go back to your company and bring out a number of new teas using your "Constant Comment" look."

Well, that answer came as a bit of a jolt because we had always thought "Constant Comment" should have its own look and any other teas we might bring out should have a totally different look. But in the face of this threat, and with the outcome still in doubt, we took his suggestion and over that winter, we developed a number of new teas—Earl Grey, Plantation Mint®, Lemon Lift®, Cinnamon Stick®, English Teatime® and a few others. Each would now have the same look as "Constant Comment" with the only difference being that the center panel of the package design on each tea would have its own distinct color (silver for Earl Grey, green for Plantation Mint®, etc.).

A true variety of teas.

In the spring of 1974, we introduced this new line to the trade. It was an immediate success and truly a turning point both for our company as well as for tea sections in supermarkets everywhere. Now tea drinkers were going to be offered a true variety of teas. Where one specialty tea had succeeded, could others follow suit? The answer would be yes. Exposure on the grocery shelf was partly responsible—we now occupied three to four feet instead of ten inches—so we definitely got noticed more. But we were also discovering that tea drinkers were responding to the concept of more variety. Within two years of the introduction of what we were now calling our "Special Blends," our business would double. What a huge bonus from an event that initially seemed so threatening. Incidentally, our competitor with his look-alike package was told to cease and desist by the court. We were very grateful!

Bigelow tea bag production line circa 1975.

The original Foodservice dispenser boxes in wire rack display.

By the late seventies, the Bigelow Tea Company had grown considerably. Our teas were now selling briskly in supermarkets from coast to coast. We had made substantial additions to our original building (page 52) and now had twenty-six tea bag machines filling thousands of canisters of our various flavors every day.

Ideas come from everywhere and anywhere. In business it is imperative to be always looking for that next big idea. This idea, which truly transformed our company started very simply with a visit by my wife Eunice and I to a college cafeteria at, of all places, the University of Hawaii. The food and beverage manager, a tea drinker thank goodness, had decided he wanted to liven up his tea service by serving a variety of teas. To do this he had gone out and bought five different Bigelow teas in a retail store, opened the canisters, put the tea bags in large apothecary jars and placed the jars right where the hot water outlet was on his cafeteria line. Each jar was labeled with the name of the tea, "Constant Comment", Earl Grey, English Teatime®, Plantation Mint® and Cinnamon Stick®. The students and faculty loved the idea of a selection. The concept was a big success. When we saw it, all we could say was "Wow, what a great idea."

But how could we reproduce this concept into something practical, something that we could ship to other college cafeterias all set up and ready to go.

We couldn't use apothecary jars, they had all kinds of obvious drawbacks, breakage, too heavy, etc. So we decided on light chip-board boxes filled with loose tea bags featuring a big label to designate the tea and a jaw-like opening that pulled down into which the tea bags spilled. We also created an attractive metal rack on which the boxes could sit. The rack helped to organize and set off the concept to best advantage.

With this idea in hand, we found ourselves entering a whole new world. Up until this point, we had only thought about selling our teas in retail stores. There had never been any thought

Foodservice line today.

Contemporary foodservice
Wire Display Rack.

to selling our teas to cafeterias, restaurants, hotels, what is called "out of home," otherwise known as food service. Our great little idea, although popular wherever we were fortunate enough to place it, was by no means an overnight sensation. It would take many years of persistence and stellar salesmanship to gain a foothold in this very different business.

It's really quite remarkable that one chance encounter can bring such enormous change to a company, but that is exactly what happened on that one short visit to the University of Hawaii. As a result millions of Americans who might never have known about us became acquainted with our teas as they find them available in the offices where they work, the cafeterias and restaurants where they dine and the hotels where they stay. What a tremendous boost this has given our business.

The Italian Individual Overwrap Tea Bag Machine.

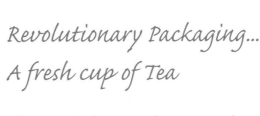

Revolutionary Packaging...
A fresh cup of Tea

Once again fate was about to step in and present us with an opportunity. This would change everything about the way we packed our teas and also open a course of future growth that we could never have achieved otherwise. It just so happened that a major packaging firm in Italy had been developing for a number of years a revolutionary new tea bag machine—one that not only filled the tea bag and attached the string and tag, but also, most importantly, overwrapped each tea bag in a fully sealed flavor protecting pouch.

When we were first presented with this machine in 1978, all of us, our executive committee as well as Eunice and myself, were somewhat confounded.

Individual fresh pack

This machine was something of an electronic marvel but we didn't know anything about electronics. Not only that, but each machine cost a small fortune—ten times more than we had ever spent on a tea bag machine.

Except for one of our management team, we pretty much rejected the concept. This machine was way too complicated and, besides which, we couldn't afford it. But the nay sayers were forgetting something—a very critical bottleneck to our future growth.

With the unwrapped tea bags we were then producing, we were committed to packing them in a canister for flavor protection. This new machine producing individually overwrapped, flavor protected tea bags made it possible to place

The first line converted to individual fresh pack envelopes.

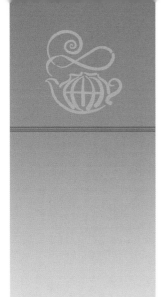

the tea bags in a flat folding box that would be formed and filled on the line at the time of manufacture.

The individually wrapped tea bag, my wife Eunice reminded all of us, would free our company from our dependency on the canister. No more warehouses bulging at the seams with space-consuming canisters. And so it was decided to buy our first overwrap machines. Over the next ten years, the canister was retired as the package of choice to be replaced by the folding box.

With our tea bags now sealed in flavor protecting envelopes, we could pursue a new opportunity… herbal teas. All natural and caffeine free, herb teas had a strong appeal for many health-conscious Americans. Once again, our research and development department came through and in 1979 we brought out eight herbal teas. Our first herbal tea entries had names like Take A Break, Early Riser and Feeling Free. Eventually over time, more generic names like Cozy Chamomile®, Mint Medley®, Orange & Spice and Sweet Dreams® would prevail. Once again the Bigelow franchise on the grocery shelf had grown.

The folding box replaces the canister in the 1980's.

With our new herbal teas as well as some decaffeinated versions of our standards ("Constant Comment", Earl Grey and English Teatime®), the Bigelow brand was now occupying *eight to twelve feet* of shelf space. We were a definite presence in the tea section— definitely getting noticed more and more — and definitely enjoying increased sales. Other major tea companies, observing the

The Merwin Street facility from above shows the many additions that were added over 33 years.

success we were having were also coming into the tea section. The black tea brands were definitely feeling threatened.

As we entered the eighties, the Bigelow Tea Company was truly growing. Over the years, Eunice and I had worked hard to build a good staff to manage our business. We were blessed with having some very fine people to whom most of our success must be attributed. More would join us in the years to come.

Our two daughters, Lori and Cindi were beginning to show an interest in the company. Lori joined us in the seventies and with her natural bent for tea and flavoring, eventually found her way to Research and Development. Over the years her creativity in the lab has given our company dozens of new and wonderful teas. She has also worked tirelessly as a Director on the Board of the U.S. Tea Association for many years.

Cindi and Lori Bigelow

Cindi, who joined our company in the eighties, has worked and also held down management positions in the other three divisions of our company, namely: Finance, Operations, Sales & Marketing. Over her twenty years with the company, she has truly learned the inner workings of the Bigelow Tea Company. She has brought new direction, great creativity and drive.

Boise, Idaho

Louisville, Kentucky

With our Norwalk plant at full capacity, it was decided in 1983 to open a packing plant in Boise, Idaho. With tea bag machines at that location, our concept was that we would blend the tea in Norwalk, ship the blended tea in 50lb foil lined paper sacks to the Boise plant and they would make the tea bags and distribute the finished cases to all of our customers on the West Coast.

We decided to make the same move a few years later in Louisville, Kentucky. Both plants have been outstanding for us, producing fine quality and giving excellent service to our many customers.

In the late eighties, my wife and I had to make something of a gut-wrenching decision. After some thirty years, we had outgrown our Norwalk plant. Office space for new people was virtually nonexistent and our tea blending facility was totally antiquated. We were going to have to move. Fortunately, in the mid-eighties, we had bought an old warehouse on a 3.5 acre site in Fairfield, CT which we were using as a distribution center. This seemed the logical place to go because we could hold on to our Norwalk staff -- it was fifteen minutes up the interstate and we could also attract people from the towns to the north and east of us. With the able assistance of an outstanding engineering and design firm, and the dedicated effort by many members of our staff, our beautiful headquarters facility was completed and we moved from Norwalk in 1990.

Corporate Headquarters
Fairfield, Connecticut

The Fairfield facility incorporates our Sales & Marketing Division, our Finance Division with its information technology group, our Operations Division which manages all purchasing, production scheduling and transportation and our Tea Division which is responsible for creating and producing our extensive variety of teas.

Direct marketing catalog

A state-of-the-art, fully computerized tea blending facility is at the core of our Fairfield building. It features four independently operated three story blending towers where we produce over eighty varieties of Bigelow teas.

The nineties were an exciting time, too. A Direct Marketing program was begun in 1993, giving consumers an opportunity to buy directly from the company. With a substantial web site (www.bigelowtea.com), as well as a beautiful annual catalog, we are reaching out to consumers across the world, offering a wide selection of tea gifts suitable for so many occasions. Today, the company has its own call center with operators standing by to take orders. We also have a fabulous facility about a mile from our headquarters where we produce many of our gifts and also fulfill thousands of orders every year.

In recent years, we have also developed a line of Vanilla based teas, Chai teas and White teas. But it is the Green tea experience that has truly helped to drive the Bigelow Tea Company for the last fifteen years. Beginning in 1990, with scientific studies showing significant health benefits to be derived from drinking green tea, the public acceptance of green tea has just been enormous. For our part, we have pursued this new

Our outstanding Green Tea.

opportunity, producing an excellent green tea, decaffeinated green tea, as well as several green teas with delicious flavors. Both at retail and food service, Bigelow Tea now plays a significant role in satisfying this demand.

Today Bigelow Tea is recognized as a leading brand in the tea industry by the trade and by millions of consumers. Today's tea drinker has come to expect the quality and taste that my mother pioneered over sixty years ago. The revolutionary packaging we introduced to tea drinkers throughout the United States in the late 1970s is recognized as the standard for the specialty tea category. At Bigelow Tea we continue to do everything in our power to make certain that yours is a perfect cup of tea!

Bigelow Tea packaging today.

The fields at Charleston
Tea Plantation.

CHARLESTON
TEA
PLANTATION

The Charleston Tea Plantation

In 2003 fate, once again, as it had done so many times before, brought us to a crossroad. The little known Charleston Tea Plantation was up for sale. Located on Wadmalaw Island just twenty-five minutes from downtown Charleston, South Carolina, it consisted of 127 acres on which were growing over 200,000 tea bushes. Thanks to the combination of high heat, extreme humidity and ample rainfall, tea cultivation is possible in what is called the "lowcountry" surrounding Charleston. Founded in 1960, the Charleston Tea Plantation is one of a kind…the ONLY tea plantation in all of North America.

The story began with a phone call from one of the owners, someone our family had been friends with for over thirty years. He asked if we would be willing to come to the rescue. After eighteen years of operation, he explained, he and his partner could no longer make a go of it and were going to have to close the gates. The plantation would soon be up for auction by the bank. We knew nothing about growing tea; much less running a farm, but our friend assured us that were we to be successful at auction, he would continue working with us. His credentials were impeccable; his knowledge of tea tasting and tea growing was vast.

But the rest of the story was bleak. There were virtually no assets other than the acreage and the tea bushes. There was an old factory building, a tea harvesting machine and a brand of tea, "American Classic" that the two co-owners had been making and selling to local grocery chains for some eighteen years. The problem here was that they hadn't produced any tea in several years. "American Classic" tea had been out of stock in the local stores for a long time. As we came to learn much later, it was very popular and had been sorely missed by a great many people. When we added it all up, there was a fair amount of money

American grown tea.

The "Green Giant"

The Charleston
Tea Plantation
Welcoming Sign

The Charleston Tea Plantation Trolley

going out and no money coming in. Our first impulse was obviously to say no. To add to the problem, the prevailing bid at auction we were told was liable to be fairly high because there were two other interested parties, one of whom was a real-estate developer. When we heard the word "developer", our tea instincts kicked in. Our oldest daughter, Lori, was particularly concerned. She felt that, as good tea people, we couldn't stand by and watch this one of a kind "gem" disappear. The thought of those tea bushes being tilled into oblivion so that another real-estate development might take their place was just too much for all of us to bear!

But how could we justify this purchase? How could we make this beautiful farm financially healthy? The answer didn't lie in the tea. Even if we sold all the tea the plantation could produce, there would still be a major shortfall of income. How about tourism? Our friend told us that over the eighteen years they had run the business, there had been significant interest in the farm shown by both local residents as well as tourists. In many instances, bus loads of people had come out to the plantation to enjoy the beautiful setting as well as to hear lectures and see demonstrations on how tea is made. We were told they loved it.

After some soul searching, we decided to say "yes". If nothing else, we would have the satisfaction of having saved this remarkable place from destruction. Once gone, this plantation would never be again. Tourism, we decided, would have to be the answer to making this farm a going proposition. After all, wasn't the city of Charleston one of the top tourist destinations in the U.S.?

The Charleston Tea Plantation Nursery

And so it was that Eunice and I went to the auction and, as predicted, the bidding was fast and furious. We had agreed beforehand

The "Tourway"

Front porch and factory

on a price beyond which we were not going to go and that figure was coming up fast. Fortunately, not too far from our top number, the other parties dropped out. We had "bought the farm" in a manner of speaking. It was a very proud moment for many of us at the Bigelow Tea Company. We had become quite attached to the idea of saving this rare piece of real estate.

Today, we're happy to report that the Charleston Tea Plantation is alive and well and thriving in America. "American Classic Tea" is back in the local stores and selling very well. It is a remarkably popular product with a very unique and delicious flavor all its own. In addition, the plantation has a brand new factory equipped with the latest state of the art tea making equipment. More importantly, the tea factory features a 150 foot long glassed in gallery perched three feet above the production floor where, as visitors stroll along, they can observe all the different processes that it takes to make tea. And, in case we're not making tea on any given day, we have three large TV screens mounted along the gallery that demonstrate the entire tea making process.

In addition, there is a beautiful gift shop where you can sample "American Classic Tea" iced tea as well as find lots of lovely tea related items. For those who want to see tea bushes up-close and personal, we have an old-fashioned style trolley that will take you on a ride around the farm.

The Charleston Tea Plantation Gift Shop

One final note. We opened in mid-2006 and as of the middle of 2008, we are rapidly approaching our 100,000th visitor. The plantation is slowly moving toward financial stability. That's certainly good news. But the best news of all is that tea drinkers from everywhere are getting to see a tea bush for the first time, taking the tour and learning things they never knew about their favorite beverage. They're loving the gift shop, and for that matter, the whole experience. We believe that over time, the Charleston Tea Plantation will become a must-see destination for tea lovers from all over the world.

Typical tea plantation

How Tea Is Made

Tea is a fascinating beverage. A miracle of nature, tea comes from a bush that's a relative of and looks very much like the camellia plant. In fact, the tea bush is called *Camellia Sinensis*. It's a sturdy plant that grows well in areas where there's a long, hot summer season and lots and lots of moisture. You'll find tea growing in China, Japan, India and Sri Lanka. It grows in parts of Russia, Turkey, Indonesia, West Africa and South America. The United States has its very own tea plantation in Charleston, SC.

The tea bush without pruning will grow into a twenty to thirty foot tree. On tea estates worldwide it is maintained at a height of some forty inches and usually in hedge rows some 45 inches wide and hundreds of feet long. Although it does produce tea pods for reproduction, generally new plants are created with five inch cuttings taken from existing plants, potted and placed in a nursery. It will take five years for the tea plant to grow to maturity. A tea plant can be productive for hundreds of years.

Tea is produced from the new growth on top of the tea bush that flushes every two or three weeks during the growing season.

Tea is produced from the new growth on top of the tea bush. This flush, as it is called, occurs every two or three weeks during the growing season. Perhaps that kind of growth is hard for you to conceive of but imagine - the days are incredibly hot - at least 100 degrees, there's a lot of moisture in the air (probably close to 100% humidity every day) and the soil is very fertile. New growth, known in tea circles as two leaves and a bud, is primarily picked by hand. In as much as the ratio of raw leaf to finished tea is five to one, some 30 *billion* pounds of leaf

Withering Bed

Rotor-Vanes

must be picked to satisfy the world's annual production of 6 billion pounds of finished tea. At any moment during the nine month growing season there are millions and millions of people employed hand picking tea all over the world.

There are three basic forms of tea - all come from the same tea bush but differ in flavor by the way the tea is processed after the leaves have been picked. The three types are known as black tea (fully fermented), oolong tea (semi-fermented) and green tea (no fermentation at all).

Although there has been a surge in green tea popularity here in the United States in recent years, black tea is far and away what most Americans consume whether hot or iced. So let's talk about black tea first.

At our Charleston Tea Plantation, making black tea is a process that involves six steps. First, after the tea leaves have been picked, they are laid out on giant wire mesh belts to a depth of twelve inches. This is called a withering bed. Warm air is circulated from below up through the leaves as they sit on the belt for some 18 hours. During this

Oxidation Bed

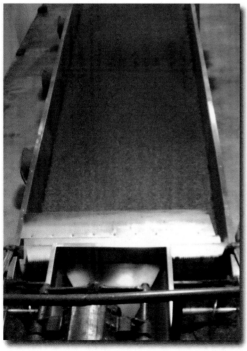

step the tea leaf wilts and loses some 15% of its moisture. Next, the leaves are put through a machine called a Rotor-Vane. Inside a cylindrical chamber which contains high speed rotating vanes, the leaves are torn, and broken into millions of tiny pieces. Once the tea leaf has been crushed and torn, the broken leaves are laid out in troughs to a depth of 2-3 inches. In this step the tea will move extremely slowly along a moving belt for some fifty minutes during which time the interaction of the air with the juices from the broken leaf oxidize the leaf and turn it from a green color to a brownish color. This process is referred to as fermentation and basically is creating the flavor that has come to be known as black tea.

Dryer Room

Leaf moving towards the dryer room.

We sift carefully to remove all stalk and fiber. We want only the pure tea leaves.

Three more steps are still to come before we have finished tea. The first is drying. Once the leaves are fermented, they fall onto a moving belt that takes them into a long oven. Here, at a heat of some 250° for 20 minutes, all fermentation stops. The moisture will completely leave the leaves and each tiny piece will shrivel up into a tight little ball. All the good flavor is now sealed in and will not be released until furiously boiling water is poured onto it. Only with boiling water will the leaf unfurl and release all its rich color and robust flavor into the cup.

Sifting is the fifth step in the manufacturing of tea. Here the tea is passed across various size screens to remove all stalk and fiber. Also in this step we pass the tea under rollers where static electricity removes the tiniest impurities.

Before we come to the sixth step, let's describe the other two basic types of tea - Oolong and Green.

Oolong tea is known as a semi-fermented tea. Oolong tea follows the same process as black tea with one exception… the time on the fermentation bed is *fifteen* minutes rather than fifty. The result in the cup is much lighter in color than black tea and the flavor is nuttier and more delicate. Typically, you will find Oolong tea served in Chinese restaurants.

Static belts with heat lamps remove the tiniest pieces of stalk and fiber.

Here comes our beautiful finished tea.

As for green tea, the fermentation process is eliminated. The tea leaf after it is picked is immediately steamed, then broken and quickly fired in the oven. The finished product retains a greenish color and produces in the cup a very pale liquoring and very delicate flavor.

In the last step all finished teas are sent to the lab for tasting. There the tea will be evaluated for color, body and flavor. If any one of these qualities is lacking, the tea taster will select other teas with offsetting characteristics to blend with that tea so as to bring it up to standard. Once all of the steps are completed, the tea is ready to go to market.

The History of Tea

Tea dates back some 4700 years to 2700 B.C. Nobody knows how tea was first discovered but legend has it that the Chinese Emperor Shen Nung was sitting one night by a campfire having water boiled for him in a large pot when some leaves from a nearby bush fell into the kettle. He was so taken with the flavor that these leaves imparted to his evening beverage that he insisted on their use from that point on. And so tea was discovered. Whether there's any truth to that legend we'll never know, but suffice it to say that around 2437 B.C. the first mention of tea in writings of that time appear. From China, tea spread to Japan probably around 600 A.D. In these two countries tea was revered for what the people in those times perceived as its many health benefits. Tea was also looked upon as being somewhat mystical and formed the basis of many occult occasions, including of course, the famous Japanese Tea Ceremony.

Tea was first discovered by the West in 1600 around the time of Marco Polo, when adventurous Portuguese and Dutch merchant vessels sailed down the west coast of Africa, around the dangerous Cape of Capricorn, out across the Indian Ocean and finally discovered China. Eventually, they began to bring back tea to the Continent and to England where it became unusually popular. When, in the 1700's, an extraordinarily high luxury tax was placed on both tea and coffee in England, many Englishmen resorted to smuggling tea. In some ways the popularity of tea in England could have been enhanced because it was considered "forbidden fruit."

Clipper ships reduced the voyage from China to the continent from six months to ninety days.

The Boston Tea Party

By 1773, tea drinking was as popular in American homes as it was in Britain and so it was that Americans were outraged by the imposing of high taxes on tea by the English government. Fueled further by the lack of American representation in the British Parliament ("no taxation without representation") some 60 men disguised as Indians boarded ships in Boston Harbor owned by the British East India Co. in December of that year. Once aboard, they smashed open the tea cargoes packed in wooden chests and threw them overboard. Other ports followed suit; and every patriotic American gave up tea drinking and turned to coffee. This incident was one of the sparks that set off the American Revolution.

In the early 1800's, Anna, 7th Duchess of Bedford, is reputed to have originated the idea of "Afternoon Tea". She conceived the idea of having tea around four or five in the afternoon to ward off the hunger pangs between lunch and dinner. (In those days dinner was served quite late). Some time earlier, the Earl of Sandwich had the idea of putting a filling between two slices of bread. These habits soon became a good reason for social gatherings, and started a trend that is still an integral part of British Life.

Tea shops were very popular in England in the 1800's. They were partly responsible for women's emancipation in Britain as an unchaperoned lady could meet friends in a teashop without bespoiling her reputation. As the popularity of tea spread, it also became an essential part of people's entertainment outside the home. By 1832 an evening spent dancing or watching fireworks in Vauxhall or Ranelagh Gardens would be rounded off by serving tea. Tea gardens then opened all over the country on Saturdays and Sundays, with the serving of tea the high point of the afternoon.

One of America's contributions to the history of tea... the tea bag.

St. Louis World's Fair 1904

Dancing was included as part of the day's festivities, so from the tea gardens came the idea of the tea dance, which remained fashionable in Britain until World War II when they disappeared from the social scene.

America has made two significant contributions to the history of tea. The first was the tea bag which was discovered quite by chance when a tea merchant decided that rather than send tea samples in the customary foil-line paper sacks, he would send his in small gauze bags. Much was his surprise when he found out that his customers, rather than removing the tea from the bags, were placing the gauze bag, tea and all, in their tasting pots. Voila-the idea for the tea bag was born.

America's second contribution to tea's history was iced tea. The year was the summer of 1904. The site-the St. Louis World's Fair. Here again, a tea merchant was offering fair-goers hot tea, but with the weather a sweltering 100°, there were no takers. An enterprising fellow, he located some ice, added it to his tea and in no time found himself swamped with people wanting to try this new found beverage.

The Charleston Tea Plantation, the only tea estate in all of North America.

Today 85% of all tea consumed in America is in the form of iced tea. Curiously, the United States is the *only* country in the entire world where iced tea is popular.

Tea grows in some 34 countries around the world. Vast tea plantations exist in India, Sri Lanka, China, Japan, Africa and South America. America also has its very own, the Charleston Tea Plantation, the only tea estate in all of North America. Located just a few miles from Charleston, South Carolina, visitors can see hundreds of thousands of tea bushes in the fields as well as witness the entire tea making process from leaf to cup in an exciting, new, air-conditioned exhibition gallery.

Today, 4700 years later, tea is the world's most popular beverage after water. With some 6 billion pounds of tea produced each year, that's enough tea for 200 cups of tea for every man, woman and child alive today. In addition to great quantities that we consume here in the United States, tea is extremely popular throughout the British Isles, Europe, Russia, N. Africa, the Mid East, the Near East and the Far East and down under to Australia and New Zealand. Some three to four billion people consume tea every day throughout the world.

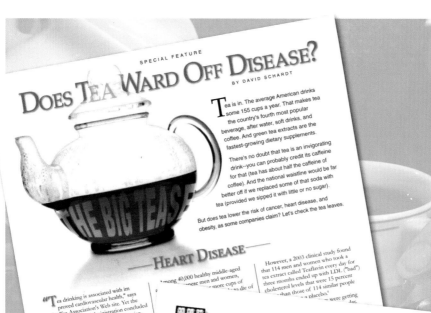

SPECIAL FEATURE

DOES TEA WARD OFF DISEASE?

BY DAVID SCHARDT

Tea is in. The average American drinks some 155 cups a year. That makes tea the country's fourth most popular beverage, after water, soft drinks, and coffee. And green tea extracts are the fastest-growing dietary supplements.

There's no doubt that tea is an invigorating drink--you can probably credit its caffeine for that (tea has about half the caffeine of coffee). And the national waistline would be far better off if we replaced some of that soda with tea (provided we sipped it with little or no sugar).

But does tea lower the risk of cancer, heart disease, and obesity, as some companies claim? Let's check the tea leaves.

HEART DISEASE

"Tea drinking is associated with improved cardiovascular health," says the Tea Association's Web site. Yet the Food and Drug Administration concluded last year that "there is no credible scientific evidence" that green tea can reduce the risk of heart disease. (The evidence for black tea isn't good, either.)

Who's right?

"It's confusing when you look across all the epidemiological studies," says tea researcher David Maron of the Vanderbilt Heart Institute in Nashville, Tennessee. "Some studies find that drinking tea is linked to less cardiovascular disease, some do not, and some actually find increased risk from drinking tea."

Clearly, the Tea Association isn't confused. According to the industry group's Web site, a University of North Carolina analysis of more than a dozen published studies "found an average estimated 11 percent lower rate of heart disease among study participants who drank three or more cups of tea per day."

The tea folks fail to disclose that the studies' results were so contradictory that, statistically, the 11 percent decrease was no different from a zero reduction.

But what if three cups a day isn't enough? Apparently, neither the Tea Association nor the researchers who looked at the health...

However, a 2003 clinical study found that 114 men and women who took a tea extract called Teaflavin every day for three months ended up with LDL ("bad") cholesterol levels that were 15 percent lower than those of 114 similar people who were getting a placebo. ... day.

... among 40,000 healthy middle-aged Japanese men and women, ... more cups of ... in ... of ...

News Release
Harvard Medical School Office of Public Affairs

Heart Attack Patients May Benefit From Drinking Tea

Boston--May 6, 2002--Drinking tea on a regular basis may help protect patients with existing cardiovascular disease, according to a study in the May 7 issue of *Circulation: Journal of the American Heart Association*, which finds that tea consumption is associated with an increased rate of survival following a heart attack.

"The health benefits of tea have been reported in numerous studies in recent years, but among healthy individuals the evidence [of tea 's benefits] is actually mixed," notes the study's lead author Kenneth J. Mukamal, MD, MPH, of the Division of General Medicine and Primary Care at Beth Israel Deaconess Medical Center. "The greatest benefits of tea consumption have been found among patients who already have cardiovascular disease."

Mukamal and his co-authors found that among individuals who had suffered heart attacks, those who reported being heavy tea drinkers had a 44 percent lower death rate than non-tea drinkers in the three-and-a-half years following their heart attacks, while moderate tea drinkers had a 28 percent lower rate of dying when compared with non-tea drinkers.

The key to this protection appears to lie with a group of antioxidants known as flavonoids, which are plentiful in both black and green tea. Flavonoids, which are also found in certain fruits and vegetables, including apples, onions and broccoli, could be working to help the heart in one of several ways, according to Mukamal, also an assistant professor of medicine at Harvard Medical School.

"It's pretty clear that flavonoids can prevent LDL [low density lipoprotein] cholesterol from becoming oxidized," he says, explaining that oxidized LDL can lead to the development of atherosclerosis. In addition, a recent study found that drinking black tea improved endothelial function - the ability of the blood vessels to relax - in cardiac patients. Finally, he adds, flavonoids may have an anti-clotting effect.

The observational study was made up of 1,900 individuals, both men and women mainly in their 60s, who were questioned by trained interviewers an average of four days after suffering a heart attack and asked to report how much caffeinated tea they typically drank each week. The participants were then separated into three groups: non-drinkers, moderate tea drinkers (fewer than 14 cups per week) and heavy tea drinkers (14 or more cups per week).

Based on these criteria, 1,019 patients were categorized as nondrinkers; 615 were moderate tea drinkers; and 266 were considered to be heavy drinkers. The patients were followed up 3.8 years later, at which time 313 individuals had died, mainly from cardiovascular disease. After accounting for differences in age, gender, and clinical and lifestyle factors, the researchers found an inverse relationship between tea consumption and mortality.

"What was surprising was the magnitude of the association," says Mukamal. "The heaviest tea drinkers had a significantly lower mortality rate than non tea-drinkers."

As is the case with any observational study, he notes, these findings could be accounted for by differences in lifestyle other than tea drinking. "One of the biggest potential criticisms of this study is that people who drink tea might be expected to live healthier lifestyles than people who don't drink tea," he explains. "But among this particular group - people mainly in their 60s who had suffered heart attacks - tea consumption was not strongly related to lifestyle." In other words, the participants were similar in terms of education, income, exercise habits, and smoking and drinking habits whether they drank a lot of tea or no tea at all.

Mukamal does caution, however, that although these findings strongly suggest that tea consumption reduces the risk of death following a heart attack, controlled clinical studies will need to be conducted to firmly establish the link.

The study was supported by grants from the National Heart, Lung and Blood Institute, the National Institute on Alcohol Abuse and Alcoholism and from the American Heart Association.

Study co-authors include Malcolm Maclure, ScD, and Jane B. Sherwood, RN, of the Harvard School of Public Health; James E. Muller, MD, of Massachusetts General Hospital; and Murray A. Mittleman, MD, DrPH, of Beth Israel Deaconess Medical Center.

Beth Israel Deaconess Medical Center is a major patient care, research and teaching affiliate of Harvard Medical School and a founding member of CareGroup Healthcare System. Beth Israel Deaconess is the third largest recipient of National Institutes of Health research funding among independent U.S. hospitals.

Tea is Healthy

You may be aware of an increased number of studies proclaiming the benefits of drinking tea. After all, it makes sense since tea is a plant which naturally contains large amounts of antioxidants. Antioxidants are like super body guards, protecting our bodies from the harmful effects of things like pollution, smoking, certain foods or sun exposure. Recent studies indicate that tea's antioxidants may aid in the building blocks of our immune system as well as possibly playing a role in reducing the risk of certain cancers and heart disease. Health studies have shown these benefits can be derived from drinking either Black, Green or Oolong tea. All three are great for you.

Here is how to steep the perfect cup of tea.

First, it is important to keep in mind that good tasting water is vital to a good cup of tea. When using tap water, always clear the stale water in your pipes by running the water a half minute before filling your kettle. If the water in your area is highly treated, use bottled water.

Brewing tea

Always bring the cold, fresh water to a rolling boil and pour it immediately over the tea. Using water that is just "hot" won't do. It must be "boiling" because the boiling water unlocks all the good flavor of tea. And finally, allow the tea to steep... about a minute in the cup and three to five minutes in the teapot depending on how strong you like your tea. Herbal teas will need more time.

So now that you understand how the various kinds of tea come to be, we urge you to go out into the vast world of tea and discover all the many wonderful teas that are available to you. Be experimental. Tea is a wonderful gift to you from nature. Whether it's a quiet moment that you seek or a need for invigoration, tea satisfies. A really fine cup of tea is one of life's true pleasures.

One More Way...
My Mother Loved Tea

My mother truly revolutionized America's concept and taste for tea with "Constant Comment". But as she continued to work on and develop the business, she came to realize that her tea worked very nicely outside the cup!

My mother started using brewed tea as an ingredient in many of the foods she prepared at home. One of her favorites, and the recipe that has stood the test of time was her great tasting "Constant Comment" Tea Holiday Punch. This punch was served throughout the holiday season at the Bigelow home. In short order it also became "the" beverage at the company's holiday social events. "Constant Comment" Tea Holiday Punch combines ginger ale, lemonade, orange and pineapple juices with fresh brewed "Constant Comment" Tea. Top that off with orange sherbet and garnish with mint leaves, and you have a great tasting and eye opening presentation for all occasions.

"Constant Comment"® Tea Holiday Punch

Ingredients:

4 cups water

4 Bigelow "Constant Comment"® tea bags

2 quarts ginger ale

2 6-oz. cans frozen lemonade concentrate

2 6-oz. cans frozen orange juice concentrate

1 8-oz. can crushed pineapple with juice

1 10-oz. jar cherries (optional)

2 pints orange sherbet

Mint leaves

Yield: 25 4-oz servings

Instructions:

In a saucepan, bring water to boil, add tea bags, cover and steep for 5 minutes. Squeeze and remove tea bags. Allow tea to cool; then chill.

Just before serving time, combine tea, ginger ale, juice concentrates (do not dilute), pineapple and cherries in a large punch bowl. Float scoops of sherbet on top. Garnish with mint leaves (optional).

More Ways for You to Love Our Tea

My mother would never have imagined that "Constant Comment" Holiday Punch would have led to where we are today for using Bigelow Teas as an ingredient in all types of food – for breakfast, lunch, dinner, appetizers, snacks, mixed beverages, salads and desserts. Over the years delicious and appetizing recipes have been developed in our kitchens. My wife Eunice, and I give most of the credit to our daughters, Cindi and Lori, for many of the newer recipes that are available on our web site at www.bigelowtea.com.

Here we offer a selection of the recipes that have become favorites over the years for the Bigelow Family. Try them, experiment with them and I hope you enjoy them as much as we have…just one more way that My Mother Loved Tea!

Green Tea Ginger Tea Cakes

Ingredients:

1½ cups cake flour, sifted

1 teaspoon baking soda

¼ teaspoon salt

6 Bigelow® Green tea bags

¾ cup boiling water

1 large egg

¼ cup light molasses

¼ cup corn syrup

½ cup butter, softened

½ cup light brown sugar, packed

2 teaspoons fresh ginger, grated

Glaze

1-2 tablespoons boiling water

1 Bigelow® Green tea bag

1½ tablespoons butter

1 cup icing sugar

Green Tea Anglaise (optional)

1 cup half and half cream

4 Bigelow® Green tea bags

2 egg yolks

3 tablespoons sugar

½ teaspoon vanilla extract

Yield: Serves 12

Prep Time: 50 minutes (includes prep time for glaze and anglaise)

Cook Time: 35 minutes

Instructions:

Preheat oven to 350°F. Mix flour, baking soda and salt together and set aside. Place 6 Bigelow® Green tea bags into a measuring cup and pour in boiling water. Let stand five minutes, remove tea bags and measure out ½ cup of tea. Grease the bottom and sides of 6 mini bundt pans or 1 large bundt pan, dust with flour, tilt to cover and tap out excess. Place egg in bowl and whisk until yolk and white are combined. In another bowl add molasses, corn syrup to green tea and stir to combine. In the bowl of a mixer, beat butter until creamy and smooth; add sugar, cream until the mixture is light in color and fluffy in appearance. With the mixer on medium speed, add the egg mixture 1 tbsp. at a time. Continue beating until the mixture is light and fluffy. Stir in fresh ginger. Alternating tea mixture and dry ingredients, fold in ⅓ of the dry ingredients, add ⅓ of the tea mixture and continue alternating, mixing well after each addition. Pour batter into prepared cake pans. Bake individual cakes 25-35 min. or until a cake tester comes out clean. Bake a large cake 35-40 min. Remove from oven and let cool on rack for 5-10 min. Remove from cake pans. To make the glaze: Make tea by placing green tea bag in a measuring cup; pour boiling water over bag and let stand for 5 minutes. Remove bag, add butter and let it melt, add icing sugar and combine. If glaze is too thick add a little water, if too thin add a little more icing sugar. Pour over mini cakes or larger cake. To make the Green Tea Anglaise: Place 4 green tea bags in small saucepan, add cream and simmer for 5 minutes. Remove tea bags. Whisk egg yolks with sugar and vanilla extract. Slowly add tea infused cream to egg mixture, whisking constantly, until all cream has been added. Return cream mixture to saucepan and cook over medium-low heat stirring until mixture coats the back of a spoon, about 4 min. Strain and allow to cool at room temp., about 20 min. Chill until ready to serve. To serve, spoon a pool of chilled Green Tea Anglaise in the center of a plate, add warm mini bundt or a slice of the larger bundt cake. Top with sauce and serve.

Pomegranate Muffins

Ingredients:

12 Bigelow® Pomegranate Pizzazz tea bags

2 cups (500mL) boiling water

3 cups (750mL) all-purpose flour

1 cup (250mL) sugar

1½ tablespoons (22.5mL) baking powder

¾ teaspoon (3.5mL) salt

¾ cup of vegetable oil

3 large eggs

1½ cup cooled Pomegranate Pizzazz tea from above (reserve 6 tbs. (90mL) for icing

Glaze

2 cups (500mL) icing sugar

5-6 tablespoons (75-90mL) of remaining Pomegranate Pizzazz tea

Yield: Makes 12 muffins

Prep Time: 10 minutes

Cook Time: 12-15 minutes

Instructions:

Make tea by steeping tea bags in the boiling water for 10 minutes. Remove tea bags. Set aside to cool. Preheat oven to 400°F (200°C). Line muffin pans with muffin paper liners (total of 12) and spray top of muffin pan with cooking spray. Combine flour, sugar, baking powder and salt in large mixing bowl. Whisk together oil, eggs and reserved tea in separate bowl until combined. Add the egg mixture to the flour mixture and stir until the dry ingredients are moist and blended. Do not over mix. Scoop the muffin mixture into prepared muffin pan, filling to the top of each muffin cup. Bake 12-15 minutes or until light golden brown or when a toothpick comes out clean. Remove from oven and cool for 5 minutes. Turn out the muffins and glaze.

Make the glaze by combining icing sugar and 5-6 tablespoons (75-90mL) tea. Add 1 tablespoon at a time to make a stiff icing. Ice the muffins with glaze.

"Constant Comment"®
Elegant Soft Drink

Ingredients:

4 Bigelow® "Constant Comment"® tea bags

4 cups water

1 quart lemon-lime soda or ginger ale

Lemon or lime, for garnish (optional)

Yield: Serves 6

Instructions:

Place tea bags into a heat-stable container. Pour one quart boiling water over tea bags and allow to steep 7-10 minutes. Squeeze and remove tea bags. Allow tea to cool, then chill.

To serve, combine equal parts of iced tea with lemon-lime soda or ginger ale in ice-filled glasses. Stir gently; garnish with lemon or lime, as desired.

Earl Grey
Royal Cream Puffs

Ingredients:

4 Bigelow® Earl Grey
   tea bags

½ cup boiling water

4 tablespoons butter, cut
   into pieces

½ cup all-purpose flour

2 eggs

*Royal Cream Filling

Confectioners sugar
   (optional)

Yield: Makes 8-10 servings
Prep Time: 10 minutes
Cook Time: 10 minutes
Chill Time: 2 hrs

Instructions:

Preheat oven to 425°F. In a medium saucepan, pour boiling water over tea bags. Let steep 10 minutes. Remove tea bags, squeezing out liquid. Add butter and bring mixture to a boil. Remove from heat and immediately add flour all at once. Stir vigorously with wooden spoon. Return to medium/low heat and continue to stir until mixture pulls away from sides of pan, about 1 minute. Remove from heat and add eggs, one at a time, beating well after each addition. The dough will be smooth, slightly dry and thick. Spoon dough onto greased baking sheets forming 8 to 10 large puffs. Bake 15 minutes, reduce heat to 400°F and bake an additional 15 minutes. Cut a slit in the side of each puff to allow steam to escape; turn off oven and let puffs rest 10 minutes. Remove puffs to cool on wire racks. Cool completely. Slice shells in half horizontally. Remove dough from inside. Fill with Royal Cream Filling. If desired, sift confectioners sugar over puffs. Serve immediately or refrigerate up to 3 hours.

*Royal Cream Filling: In medium bowl, pour ½ cup boiling water over 2 Bigelow® Earl Grey tea bags; let steep 10 minutes. Remove tea bags, squeezing out liquid. Stir 1½ cups well-chilled heavy cream. Add 1 package (3.4 ounces) instant vanilla pudding and pie filling mix. Beat with wire whisk 2 minutes until slightly thickened. Chill until ready to use.

"Constant Comment"® Cake

Ingredients:

½ cup milk

5 Bigelow "Constant Comment"® tea bags

½ cup unsalted butter (1 stick)

1 cup sugar

3 eggs, room temperature

1⅔ cups flour

2½ teaspoons baking powder

Confectioners sugar

Yield: One 9" round cake

Instructions:

Preheat oven to 350°F. Grease and flour a 9" round cake pan. Combine milk and tea bags in a small saucepan. Heat over medium/low heat until bubbles form around the edge, stirring occasionally. (DO NOT BOIL.) Remove from heat and let cool (15-20 minutes); remove tea bags, squeezing out liquid. Set aside. In large mixing bowl, cream butter and sugar until smooth. Add the eggs and whisk to blend. Add the cooled milk; continue to whisk until thoroughly combined. Add flour and baking powder; mix until a smooth batter forms. Pour batter into pan. Bake approximately 35 minutes, or until center of cake springs back when touched. Cool on wire rack before removing from pan. Let cool completely before serving. Dust top with confectioners sugar.

Bigelow® Vanilla Caramel Cake with Vanilla Caramel Glaze

Ingredients:

3 cups sifted flour

1 tbsp. baking powder

½ tsp. salt

8 oz. (2 sticks) unsalted butter, softened

2 cups of sugar

4 eggs

1 cup milk

6 Bigelow® Vanilla Caramel tea bags

For Vanilla Caramel Glaze

3¾ cups (1 lb.) powdered confectioners sugar

6 Bigelow® Vanilla Caramel tea bags

½ cup boiling water

Instructions:

Preheat oven to 350°F degrees. Butter and flour Bundt® cake pan. Combine milk and tea together in small saucepan and bring to a boil over medium heat. Immediately turn off heat. Steep for 6 minutes. Strain and set aside to cool. Cream the butter until smooth and fluffy. Add sugar and mix until blended. Add eggs one at a time. Add dry ingredients and tea/milk infusion to the butter mixture, mixing just to combine. DO NOT OVER MIX! Pour batter into the buttered Bundt pan. Bake until risen, golden and firm to the touch, 45-55 minutes. Let cool in the pan. Then glaze with Bigelow® Vanilla Caramel Glaze. (If making cupcakes with this batter, butter muffin pan and bake for 21-23 minutes or until toothpick inserted in the center comes out clean. Then glaze with Bigelow® Vanilla Caramel Glaze.)

To make glaze pour ½ cup of boiling water over 6 tea bags. Steep for 6 minutes. Remove tea bags, squeezing out liquid. In a large bowl, place the 3¾ cups of confectioner's sugar. Slowly add the tea by whisking vigorously until creamy.

Option 1: Bigelow's Cherry Vanilla Tea or any other of Bigelow's Vanilla Teas can be used in place of Vanilla Caramel Tea.